Lambert's

Collection of Poems for Different Occasions

SCRIPTOR HOUSE
THE EPITOME OF GREATNESS

FRANK LAMBERT

Scriptor House LLC

2810 N Church St Wilmington, Delaware, 19802

www.scriptorhouse.com

Phone: +1302-205-2043

Published by Scriptor House LLC

Paperback ISBN: 979-8-88692-256-1

eBook ISBN: 979-8-88692-257-8

Lambert's

Collection of Poems for Different Occasions

FRANK LAMBERT

Contents

To Beauty and Grace

To beauty and grace is a magnified style of
what we see when we look at someone.

Their stylish clothes, coloured hair with flair, coloured eyes
that stare from blue mirrors that we see in their eyes.

The blue eyes are soft as the sweetness
of a character that can be trust

Brown is not wrong but feels the
strength of a strong character.

The voice is stern with a love of compassion

Bugs

There are bugs of all kinds,

June bugs, water bugs, flying bugs and
some just bugs,those are called ladybugs.

There are fat ones, tiny ones, even ones that stare but don't
kill them because there are more to come and stare.

There are good bugs , bad bugs , strange ones
and sometimes there are edible ones.

There are bugs that come with a meal and there
are ones that are not allowed in your meal .

Bugs come in colour ,black .red, brown but don't frown.
I am sure there are ones that come in your colour.

Bugs become pets, strange to a vet but he is
the only one that will care for your pet.

Winter

The last months of the year brings

Snowy dreams of skating ,skiing sound like fun
but shoveling snow is not so fun.

Winter days and chilli nights glistening icicles
hanging like shining lights.

Sipping on hot tea you wonder about fond memories
of winter pass. snowy nights, fun filled nights
with someone cooking good old bread buns.

Birds that stay in winter months looking for food
in winter, bird feeders filled with favourite treats,
who knows when this will last,

Christmas carols singing in the night oh the
sound of their sweet sounds echoes for miles,
it is sure to give you a smile

Winter months go by fast ,soon spring is in the air
and those worried thoughts will disappear,

The smell of flowers will soon be here.

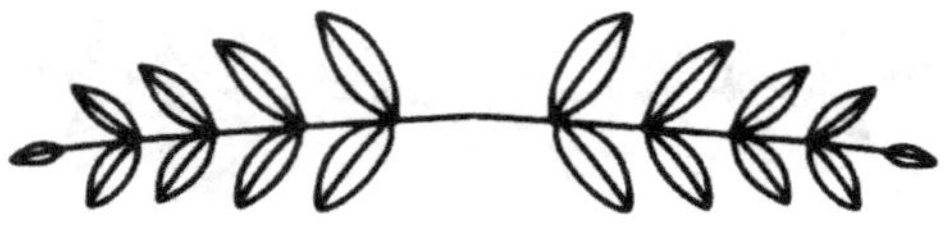

People of Culture

There are many cultures,that live in this land,

From east ,west . north and south ,some cultures
fast and some don't last ,because of the season,

Snowy, cold , hot or too much rain it's a shame.

People from different colours are all the same,

Just their colour is not the same.

Our need to care is in all of us ,so be not
ashamed of your colour,we all get into trouble .

It's the greed that exceeds wouldn't you agree.

So when you are out and about to be
kind to those of a different colour,
they are the same but with a different colour.

There are different attitudes with
cultures some good, some bad.

Some times they change and sometime not,
but it's not fair to judge by the culture or colour ,
just be kind soon you:ll like them in time

Spring is in the Air

Another year is here, spring is in the air, fresh flowers
everywhere and smiles can be seen from a mile.

New life is born, the signs are everywhere.

New buds on the trees and warmth of the air and
robins returning from the southern break.

In a blink of an eye the scenery is green,
birds sing love begins, moods swing and the
happiness is back sweet sounds of music is in the air.

All things living are embracing the music ,
and the dance of pollination alive with flare.

OH oh oh ,how we dare to sing with happy birds,
to be happy and sing from the heart, as it is a love of art.

God's spirit shines. Our spirits are reborn,
our life's energies revived, we shed our winter
malaise and look forward to summer highs.

Summer swans are a sight to see, summer festivals
are a delight, dancing in the moonlight, until midnight
happy cheers are such a delight when summer is here.

The stars and the moon provide us with light all through
the night. Mother nature embraces us throughout the day.

They all speak to our souls and stimulate our minds,
trying to show us that there's life of other kinds.

Developmental Reading Disorder

DEVELOPMENTAL READING DISORDER, ALSO CALLED **DYSLEXIA**, IS A READING DISABILITY THAT OCCURS WHEN THE BRAIN DOES NOT PROPERLY RECOGNIZE AND PROCESS CERTAIN SYMBOLS.

A POEM FOR PEOPLE THAT HAVE DYSLEXIA:

A long time ago, when children were misunderstood, the teacher asked a student to explain about a train.

The student replied, "I can't explain because I have dyslexia, but I'll try to explain. The transmitters in my brain are telling me that there are broken pieces of the track that are gone and that the signs are on the wrong side of the track, so all I see is the back side of the sign. I am sure that the train is on its tracks, but it's travelling backward out of town."

"But," said the teacher with a stunned look, "Why would there be pieces of the track missing?"

The student replied, "Maybe they are going to replace them like they are going to replace my brain, or maybe they are going to reroute my transmitters, and they should do that with the train tracks."

A Rabbit Named Hoppy

There was a bunny named Hoppy.

His ears were so floppy they would mop the floor.

His fur was soft as a feather,
people would say he would make good leather.

But Heather didn't like the thought of Hoppy
turning into a feather or a piece of leather.

Heather knew what to do,
so she turned him into a kangaroo.

So Heather trained the rabbit not to get in the habit
of being a rabbit but a kangaroo that knew what to do.

FRIDAY

F-R-I-D-A-Y is the day of the week we get paid,
but some of us just give it Away, hay-hay

So what do you say? Money

For the tax man, milk man, and
even money for the old man

That kicks the pop can.

R is for "rest" that do work your best; so take a
rest and don't

Be a pest, or you will be sleeping in a nest.

I is for "I am a fool for feeling like a tool"
because now I Can get off my stool.

D is for "done," the last day of the week.

A is for "answering my prayers" to get
through this week of work.

Y is for "why I am doing all this work for the tax man

That no one cares but the tax man?"

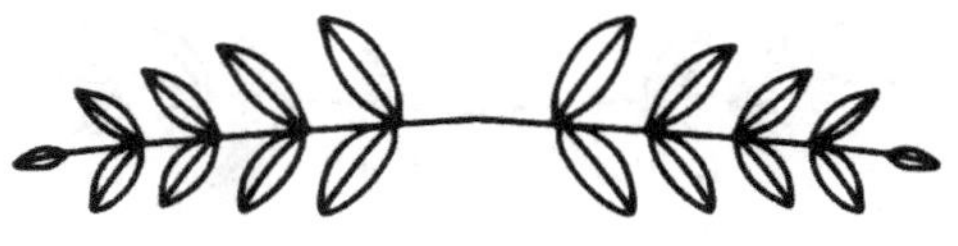

I am We are

I am you and you are me , if we choose to let it be.

I am the tree and the roots that keep me grounded.

I am the earth that gave us all the miracles of birth

I am again ,the roots that connect us to
everything and everyone .

To the light to the darkness that lives
inside of each and everyone of us.

I am the energy that we share ,Oxygen
and the love that we are a part of.

Let's take a closer look at who we really are,
look on the inside of our soul and see the
connection to the sun and very importantly,

Our connection to each other.

We are all a part of everything .

You are me and I am you

We are the earth , the trees and the entire
universe if we simply choose to let it be

Happy Birthday, Mother

Ho, Mother, dear!

How are you?

It all started in fifty-two, when you
were nineteen, and ended forty-two years later,
when you would end up with eight and still feel young.

The days were fun when there was only one.

The days were long, nights were short,
joys of happiness and tears of sadness with only one.

You prayed for the things that you knew and
worried about the things in life that you did not know.

In years to come, your worries will be free with all your
love in motherhood.

Each child would learn the love that he or she received
and give it back in the form of a gift, saying,

"Thank you, Mom. I LOVE YOU.

HAPPY BIRTHDAY!"

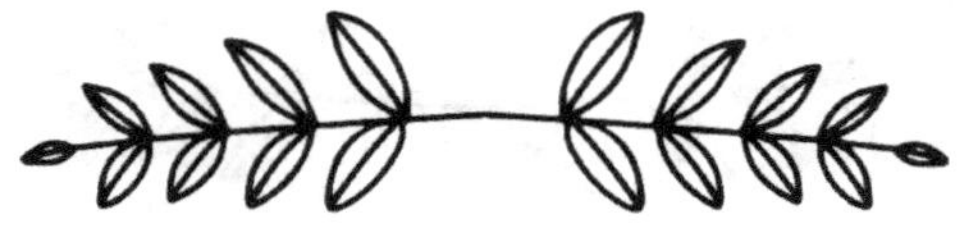

Hot Summer Days

The hot summer days are here to stay;
three months of tanning in the sun.

We discover it's a lot of fun.

Our moods change from being sad to having
glad that we are having fun in the sun.

The days are long, nights are short,
and the sea of stars twinkle at night.

When our luck runs out,
we sit and ponder with our eye sto the sky,
for those warm nights are a delight.

The warm summer nights will pass and
the cool nights will blow in.

Longer nights will show.

East-north winds blow in: sign of the year's end.

A Boy Named Nikolas

There was a boy named Nikolas. When he was two, he became a genius, and he didn't know what to do. He grew and grew right out of his size 2 shoe. Soon he was four foot two.

He said to his mommy, "I'm not going to be no dummy. I am going to be six feet four and no more because I might bump my head on top of the door. I pray to God that the door will be seven four so I will not bump my head any more."

When he became eleven, he prayed to God that is in heaven. Along came Kaitlyn who was seven; if we all pray towards heaven, we will all go to heaven.

Nikolas and Kaitlin grew up together and knew what they wanted to do. Their mommy was proud that they didn't keep their heads in a cloud. They would sing in a crowd and sound really loud.

They are with a group of seven who sing to the great heavens. Let them be loud so they can be heard above the clouds. They sing about Jesus; he is the one that sets us free from our misery.

When we get mad because someone made us sad, we turn to a note in the Holy Book. We don't read very long from the book that gives us hope before our troubles are gone. When we try to forgive, our worries are set free because we get on our knees and pray to the one that will set us free from our troubles, can't you see? Turn to your right then tune to your left; you better believe

I am right! That Jesus is the one!

Little Sister

Once upon a time, I knew a little girl; she was four foot two with blue eyes, and I watched out for her too.

When her brother was surrounded with trouble, there was double trouble because the little sister insisted she would bruise their troubles.

She would put her hands on her hips, do a little twist, and sound mean.

The trouble at hand ran; big brother shook her hand and said, "Thank you for being my little sister at hand.

The Red Morning Sky

In the early morning sunlight,
shining through the trees,
light red sky,
time stood still.

Picture moment,
the feeling of peace,
serenity, and alone but happy.

The serenity with peace,
God's spirit, and the peace on earth.

The warm comfort of the spirit that moves us
through different times of our lives brings peace,
enjoyment, and growth to our inner peace with ourselves.

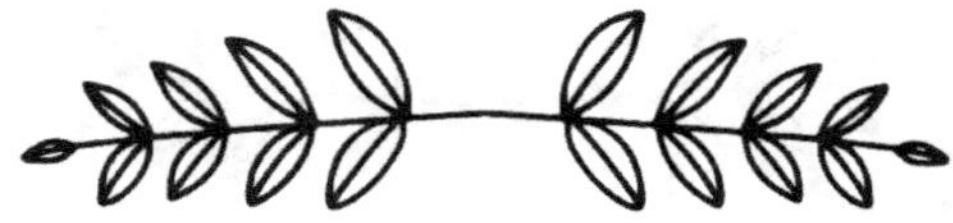

Love Affaires

In the midst of our time,
we consume dates, places,
and archiving goals.

In busy moments, we stop, stare,
and listen to people's love affairs.

Some good, some bad, and some are a mystery;
but any one of us could be in those love affairs.

When we choose to be in love,
our emotions are running wild with fears
and tears, with overassertive feelings
of not caring or overcaring.

To express our thoughts of care,
is to plan a loveing plot

In the ones we
Care to love a lot.

Man of Thought

A child is conceived into a world that is
full of grace, beauty, and peace.

The greed within drives us to an early end of what
could have become, for the sea is full of greed.

A mustard seed is small, but when it gets tall,
you can see what it can do for all.

A child that grows with beauty and grace
will make every ending a happy place.

The old will pass, and young will carry on,
for it's the life that will never end.

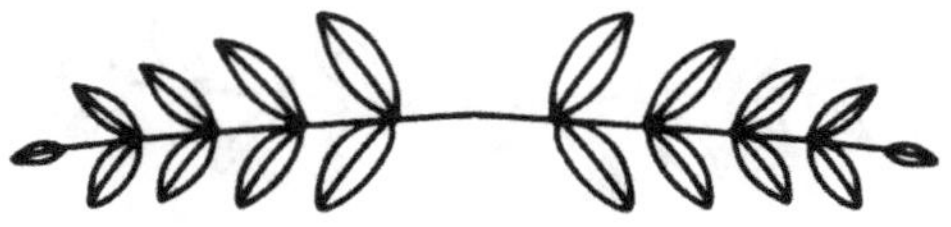

Perception of Mind

When we are young, we see softness, smoothness,
and perfection in people's faces.

Perception in perfection leads up to believing
in honesty, care, and trust.

Being distorted and mean-looking is to believe
in distrust, meanness, and unfriendliness.

The eye sees wrinkle-free, soft, and warm in the heart faces
everywhere, but only for a moment in time.

In a slow moment in time, the face
changes to a different shape.

When we are young and full of fun, our minds
and hearts still play like we are young.

The body knows when it is time to go slow.

Full Moon Delight

We are live , love and laugh under the same sun.

Noon great but the night time moon is a delight,
such as whispers in the air are shared.

Sounds are heard , some not in the air, but happy
laughter also is in the air with delight.

The delight of the full moon shines everywhere,
on earth and throughout the universe.

It ignites a magic for us to be aware of the light, it ignites
in us, and to use our power to love and to trust.

Thrust comes with time ,to those who have the time,
but don't get moonstruck because the
full moon is a devilish delight.

It lights up the path of our journey on earth.

Guides us to the hidden treasures and
impacts the miracle of birth.

The miracles that one sees, sometimes we don't
believe with wonders in our hearts with disbelief.

I choose to believe in miracles,
as that makes us grow the more we grow from our hearts,
the more we allow our love to show.

Our hearts will glow like the midnight moon that glows,
so bright and wide, others will follow angels and
sing in wondrous delight.

Heavenly sounds will envelope the earth, our hearts will
listen, our minds will calm, our eyes will see what wasn't
seen before, our inner spirit will freely soar

In Times of Getting Old

It is Friday; TGIF. O, for me it's another day with
little pay, but I got Granny, who has lots to say.

Now she is fast asleep for another day.

When ten minutes have passed, she wakes; she thinks
that she slept in her chair all night, but it has been

Ten minutes passed. Little old Granny getting ready to go
to the store, she is all ready, but before she goes,
she sits beside the door.

The last-minute rest before going out the door,
She closes her eyes to remember what she needs at the
store; before long, she is snoring at the door.

An hour has passed, and I think she is at the store, but no,
she is still at the door snoring and dreaming about the past.

When I come down to pass her, she wakes; she says, "I am
going to the store," but an hour has passed.

That is why she makes me laugh.

When old Granny has come back at last, we dine together
and have a few more laughs. Then she sits with her tea,
and she is so pleased to have me.

It is time to have more zzzzzzzz.

Now she has gone for another zzzzzzzz.

In an hour or two, she'll be calling me,
"What are you doing? It is time for snack,"
and that will put her back to dreamland once more.

In the middle of the night, she is at my bedroom door
and says, "I didn't know you were home. Well,
good night!" and that is why I laugh at night.

The poor old Granny makes me laugh, but she is all right.
She likes to check things in the middle of the night.

Old Mr. Tree

As I sit and look out my window, the trees are bare
and autumn is in the air cool days, leaves blowing
everywhere, and frost that sits on the moss.

Soon, snow will cover the moss, and the
whirling winds will blow.

Some days echo with sounds bouncing across the fields.

Every year, the old man tree grows and gets older,
and his roots grow deeper under the ground.

Old man tree stands his ground, withered by the weather as
years pass and his branches last.

Spring is here: buds blossom, green is everywhere,
and beautiful sights are a delight.

Poetry of Thought

He who fills his mind with knowledge
will have less room to worry.

He who fills his mind with worry will have more pain
to gain because he is not filling his well-being.

He who fills his soul will fulfil the dream of being satisfied.

The brain needs to exercise the thoughts
of our fruits, like a muscle to be exercised.

The eyes see beauty and grandeur.

The eyes see a picture like a piece of marble with
shades of colours of blue, green, and brown.

The ears are to hear like a voice that hears beautiful poetry.

The songs that we hear reflect a moment
in time from years that have passed.

This little note will give your brain
something to think about.

Poem of Should Not

We sit and think, ponder what we should do.

We laugh at the past, we continue with a smile for a while,
and we change our ways from looking through a haze.

There is a path that will give us grandeur at
last but sometimes it is hard to find.

The search will bring us to the end, and there, we will
pass on a beginning for someone who will
continue the path that we started at last.

When we are small, we wish we would be taller;
but in a short while, short is better after all.

Our parents get lazy and we get crazy.

When we are small, they let us crawl
all over the shopping mall.

We defied the rules that make us look cruel, but then
there are new rules, and our parents look like fools.

Our rules shape us, as I am told, but
I think it makes us feel old.

For when we look in the past for
those rules, they never last.

So in the end, we are all fools for following so many rules.

Poem of Feelings

There was a man who likes to write poems, even his own.

Most people write poems when they are alone,
and there are people at home, and they still feel alone.

Poems are from happy thoughts, sad thoughts,
and thoughts that don't mean a lot.

Poems from oppression, the Great Depression,
and from people's obsessions.

Poems are feelings of love, like a white dove that is pure.

The gentle words that go from ear to ear
and to the heart, where it stays all year.

Someone's Mother

This is a story about someone's mom in the early years.

This mom was no bum; she found a man and took his hand.

In this land they stood together hand in hand;

Soon they were having babies in the sand.

The baby came soon after a rain.

It would be clear that the baby's name would be Sam.

In no time at all, Sam grew mighty tall,
and now he plays in Carnegie Hall.

A child is like a seed: put it in the ground with lots of water
and watch it grow, and it will become mighty tall.

In the beginning, if you don't know what to do,
pick something and give it your all!

You might be playing with Sam in Carnegie Hall.

January

January!

A new start for the year.

A new start for what we will bear.

A new start to end all those grey hairs.

A new start to end last year's tears of weary
hearts and long, endless thoughts.

A new year of no more wasted fears,
just sunny skies and brave hearts.

A new start at longer days and less haze,
and no more lazy days.

February

The month that is short and sweet; the month will come
and go with less snow to show, for we will know.

The way we say hello to the snow that blows under our feet,
and we will not be defeated by the cold.

For the end of the month will show that the snow is a
sign of relief, to believe that spring is in the air.

The sweet smell of flowers, warmth of the sun, and the
happier hello with no snow to show has been won

March

The March winds roar in like a lion,
so the beast will have the last roar before
the winds of calm claim the latter part of March.

Before long, April showers will bring May flowers.

Smell of Spring

The sweet smell of different flowers is the sign of spring.

Birds sing with sweet sounds of music
that echo through the treetops.

Squirrels chirp; they chase each other up
the pole and in their hole.

Babies begin to know how to hold their toes.

Long last, winter air that flows out the door at last;
the spring breeze from the sea makes us feel free.

Season of Summer

Winter is gone and summer comes along;
the long, hot days are here to stay.

Millions of lights cast the sky at long last;
the summer nights that twinkle with delight.

Some nights the moon is full, and howling
sounds echo all through the night.

Autumn

The sea of green forestry changes to a wonder of beauty.

Rainbow colours fill the treetop with different shades.

As sun fades down, shades of beautiful
colours of leaves brighten.

Cool air makes us stare and wonder
why such beauty fades away.

The cold north winds blow in town,
and sounds of happy cheers
from summer are all gone,
and now autumn is all around.

Winter

Winter is not so nice because it's cold,
and sometimes we feel like ice.

When we sit by the fire and stare into the warm,
fiery flares, we are not ashamed of being
in the house and curling up like a mouse.

As crackly sounds come from the fireplace, the
cold east wind blows hard, and thoughts
of last summer's fun of playing in the sun.

Each cold day brings us closer
to those warm summer nights.

We are like ships that sail through stormy weather, to
embrace the bad and cherish days that are not going to last.

The wind howls, snow blows like little tornadoes across the
open fields, and, o, cold winter days are here to stay. For
we will pray for those warm summer days.

Spring

The smell of spring is the beginning, but
the end of old will soon be told.

In the moment of beauty, we ponder the perfection
of grandeur in the sight that we behold.

Blossoms in the spring fill the air with
sweetness everywhere.

The birth of a child, a flower that opens up,
puts us in a groove to get us to a better mood.

We become happy like old man Pappy, so we were told.

Our happy smile will do us a while,
for we will pray
for those days that are long and
for many nights that are short.

We will rest in our little nest for another day.

Summer

The summer sun is warm; the heat will
make your feet feel neat.

We will have fun in the sun, provided
your buns don't get burnt.

Our arms will tan when we use our hands
to make something out of sand.

Pools of water are there to wet your hair.

So when you are in doubt about being cool, you will
look more like a fool for not getting in the pool.

The summer heat will compete with you
to see how long you can stay in the heat.

Fall

Fall is the season of the year, we come to
prepare ourselves that winter is coming.

Moods that we must bear put us in hiding.

We do not want to be fooled by the cool winter air that
makes us stare and think of those warm summer nights.

The sky is thick with stars that are far: they glitter with
delight, and in a few hours, there will be sunlight.

The fall is here; colours fade with different shades,
and who is to say that each day will be a delight?

Winter Ice

Winter is here; we see soft white blankets
cover the land from where we stand.

When cars or buses go by, the soft snow blows everywhere,
for it is a scene to be seen with delight.

The trees are bare from summer wear;
the open fields are covered with snow,
and the glitter of ice from the
open fields looks so nice.

When you stop walking, sound echoes
across the land from where you stand.

The cold winter days will stay, and it will be
hard to play on those cold, frosted days.

Snow

A long time ago, when we didn't have snow,
we used to go to the show.

There were scenes of screams and scenes that should not be
seen, but the laughter lasted until late after.

The fun that we had did not make us mad or even sad.

So now we have snow, and who will know the fun that

We might have playing in the snow.

Trust and Love and Joy

The material that you see is a cloth that has different shades
of colour, and three stones: trust, laugh, and joy.

When we meet someone of different shades of colour—
from skin tones, hair tones, and facial —
we see beauty, a piece of art created in a
way that it reflects our inside perfection.

The one piece of art that interests us to a point
where we do not change but ponder the inside
of beauty that is in front of us.

How did that work of art form into a
beautiful person from the grains of sand,
from God, that gave us beauty, love, and joy?

We must make sure that beauty sustains
us for the rest of our lives.

May our journey with each other be blessed
with happiness, tears of joy, forgiveness, and trust.

Love each other always.

The Wicked Old Man

Do you have a topic for Mr. Poet?

How about a stick, wick, brick, thick, or a candlewick?

There was a wicked man who lived out of a garbage can;

His hands were thick like a brick.

His body was thin; that is why he didn't like the wind.

He would blow around like a balloon in a room.

That is why he didn't like the wind.

But along came Jim and told him he was too thin.

"That is why you should stay out of the wind."

Along came Mick with some bricks; he gave it to the
wicked old man that carried a mighty thick stick.

"Take these bricks and put them in your garbage can so
when the wind blows, you won't look like a
balloon that was blown around in a room."

The Stress and Strain

There was a man that was stressed,
so he got undressed and went in the pool to get cooled,
and the strain in his brain got fooled.

He was starting to feel great, along came a snake
and got caught up his rear, so the man put himself
in high gear, and out flew the snake from his rear.

So don't get undressed to relieve your
stress; just use your brain to relax the strain.

Take a run in the rain—that would be more fun.

O, Poet Man

O, poet man, o, poet man, o,
poet man, come rhyme with me.

My words are funny because sometimes
they come from my honey.

She believes in me to be her honey.

I make her laugh, she splits in half, and
now I have two Playboy bunnies.

People think I am insane, writing
about my good-looking dame.

But I have no shame, and I think she is great just as same.

She thinks I am cool, but she knows I am no old fool.

I make her lots of loot, but no way is she getting the boot.

Death

For this letter is hard to write, everyone
knows there is a beginning and end.

To see something or someone come to the end,
it puts tears and fears in the moment.

So we must reflect the moments of
happy times and sad times.

We must accept the people that we love and gracefully
accept their passing away, for God is in control.

We will all have our time; embrace the death but
never forget the tears and fears that hold
from the past good times and bad.

Happy Mother's Day

MY DADDY WROTE THIS TUNE,
AND IT GOES LIKE THIS:
YOU ARE EIGHTY-ONE;
YOU ARE NUMBER ONE.

Daddy says you've been a mother for sixty-two years; that
is a long time to tell your children to clean out their ears.

You say to them, "I want you to hear what I have to say and
not nod your head and continue to play in the hay.

I am getting old, as I am told, but I still can have fun
in the sun with my sons and daughters on this
special day they call Mother's Day.

Every day should be Mother's Day, that's what I say.

This day is for me.

I like to be the queen for a day—sit on a throne,
but not the one that is cold like a stone.

The one that is heated for my little tush.

So come bow in front of me, give me a hug
and a kiss, and I'll be pleased.

I promise I won't sneeze, but I will be pleased when
you all have to leave because I have to have a nap
with that old guy that you call your pappy."

Mr. Coffee

Old Mr. Coffee fell in love with Ms. Toffee;
in no time at all, out came little Hoppy.

The trio went to visit Rio and came
back with another bambino.

The colour of their skin was very thin
and different shades of brown.

So the town decided to make them one shade
of brown, so they sent them out of town.

The family decided to be a toffee shade of brown,
then they would look less like a clown.

So when the family came back to town, the toffee
shade of brown was yummy in their tummy.

So the town had a countdown for them to get out of town
because the townspeople just loved that shade of brown.

Mr. Cancer

Old Mrs. Breast was too tough for Mr. Cancer; he did his best, but old Mrs. Breast was the best.

She had two on her side: two against one will always have more fun.

She gave old Mr. Cancer a one-two punch, and now he is out for lunch.

We are the champions . . . of tomorrow . . .

Now you know, don't mess with the best because there are two that are the best.

Mr. Poet

Here I sit to think and almost turning pink;
my brain will strain until the words will
flow out like a river that flows with joy.

Your mood will change once you
hear the joys of happy tears.

From time to time, we like to pass the time from
years ago that gave us laughter and tears of sadness.

We wish we were someone else, in a different place
and time, but why not embrace the moment
of time that we are in at the moment?

To embrace is to accept something.

We are like a tree that has seen good and
bad weather that come and go.

The tree becomes deep-rooted from a seed,
and embraces but does not agree.

So when you are in troubled times, embrace and learn; just
like a ship at sea that encounters high waves, they will pass,
and the sea will be calm at last.

Man at War

O, God, bless me with words I do not understand
but people read with a big bang.

Even the gangs will stop shooting each other.

They will shake each other's hands and
listen to some great band.

In a moment or two, the gangs will understand that there is
no better man to shake with than the enemy at hand.

There is no better defeat than getting
along with your fellow man.

The world is at war when we take a stand; the soul doesn't
want a war when taking a stand, but he wants his followers
to understand to get along with his enemies at hand.

So when you get in the fighting mood, read a note
or two from the Holy Book; and before long,
your troubles will be gone.

Then go to your enemy, shake his hand, and say
I am sorry for getting out of hand because

**I LOVE IT WHEN WE STAND TOGETHER IN THIS
GREAT LAND.**

Shades of People

The streets are full of people, different sizes,
colour, culture, and style of fashion.

There are weird ones, lonely ones, colourful
ones, pitiful ones, and sad ones.

There are people that beg for their money, work for
their money, and should be given some money.

There are happy faces, sad faces, and faces with
tears of fear.

All these faces will always be here; as one fades
from the scene of the streets, another reappears.

Leaves from trees fade away when the seasons
change to different shades.

The world is a busy beehive: as one dies,
another is replaced.

So in a moment, step aside and realise the beauty
and colour that is before your eyes; enjoy the
scene from the streets that you pass by.

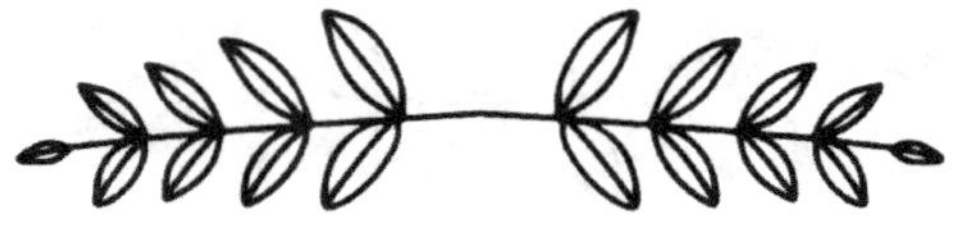

Hot Passion

There is a boy that has so much joy,
he thinks of you as his toy.

You are sweet with those cute little feet.

Your hands feel soft when he holds your hand.

You are the same height, and it is easy to
ignite your lips with hot passion.

When we kiss, I am sure I won't miss your
lips because of the height.

They always put me in flight.

We are in sync in our thinking even
when we are so far apart.

You fill my brain with less strain, and we gain happy pain
that is so delightful that the laughter goes on forever after.

We gain happy pain that is in times of despair; we share the
tears of the years that we suffer, but we grow with pain, and

now we know that we should have taken a bow towards
one another.

The time has passed, and our pain and strain is in the past.

We are free to see the future together at last, to share
those laughs from the past and to gain happiness
with each other for the future.

The long lonely nights are cold, but what we
hold in our hearts, the art of passion, is
burning with delight for each other.

When we sit and stare into each other's eyes, thoughts
of feeling a tingling is the love that is mingling
towards each other; so the next lazy day, let's play
in the hay, for we will have each other as our babe.

I pray every day that your pain is less and less;
in the time, we will gain happy pain with
love and laughter forever after.

Friendship

A long time ago, there was a man and a woman
that met each other with open eyes and
kind hearts towards each other.

As time passed, the friendship grew with love in their eyes
and passion in their hearts towards one another. As the
friendship grew, so did the space between them, but the
memories of each other never faded from their hearts.

They were at awe with each other; the past difficulties that
they encountered were way behind them.

The feelings towards each another grew stronger, and their
love began again with no difficulties.

Their goals in mind were the same: to be with each other,
to enjoy their friendship that they always wanted towards
each other.

No one knows the future of two people that care for each
other, but the hope and the passion are very strong.

Best of Friend

This is the day that I can say that your friendship means
a lot because the times have come and gone. Our laughter
and silly love songs ring in my ear, even when I
have not seen you for a whole year.

Our friendship grew out of the blue when we met
at the mall, when we both saw those cute little buns
walking through the mall. Years have passed, our
friendship has lasted.

We are older and less bolder, but our friendship has lasted;
thank you for being my friend forever after.

Father's Day

Father's Day is a special day we tell our fathers

Thanks for the love and time he spends
shaping our thoughts.

Sometimes the love is lost but will come back tenfold.

Fathers teach us how to be firm, But soft like a fern tree.

Believe in yourself like a mighty Rock but kind to
those Blind.

The father's love is like no other;

Spend time, and he may save you some dimes.

A Town That Has No Frowns

There was a girl named Nicky.

She was so picky about too many hickeys,
her man took her hand and they skipped,
danced, and kicked a tin can all the way
down to a town that had no frowns.

When they got there, the people's frowns
were nowhere to be found.

The people never got sad or mad.

They were just glad to be there.

Smiling faces in a town that has no frowns is
a happy place to hang out with a clown.

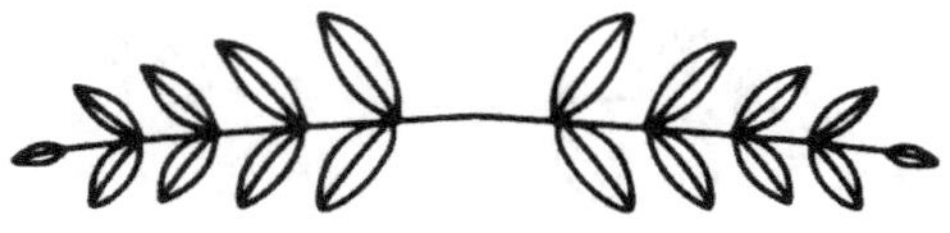

Time has Come

As we are young, we enjoy our fun playing in the sun.

The sun radiates the warmth of love,

like the softness of a white dove of pureness.

As we grow, we are told to know the glory of
the Lord that watches out for our soul.

Listen to the spirit that whispers so softy:
like a gentle breeze, his voice is stern, and you will be
pleased with the seed that was planted in you.

The love of light will shine from you, and
people will be pleased to know you.

The days that come and go, stress and tension get our
attention because of the days before are a reflection.

The air is thick of deflecting people's moods, so when the
fog thickens of people's moods, get in the groove
of moving your mind; stand your ground so the
thick fog will move around you.

Be like a mouse in a house, quiet and hidden.

The moods change like the tides of the sea.

Winds shift and moods become calm, tension is released,
air is recharged, happy smiles flare, laughter is everywhere.

Another day has come and gone;
happy thoughts come and go.

Happy thoughts, smiling faces, and
laughter are to stay for another day.

Skating Time

Once upon time, there was a girl named Nicky.

The boys liked her because they used to give her a hickey.

Beauty was her trait, but when she laced up her
skates, all the boys stood at the gate.

She was swift, even some boys gave her a lift.

Sometimes she had to refrain because
the boys were driving her insane.

The boys were cute, but some got the boot.

Some were fun, but she didn't need a gun.

The smile on their faces would last a
while on some boys' faces.

The dribbles on her face would give the boys a
bigger face, with smiles and fun that would
last a lifetime of memories in the sun.

As years faded, the memories last to this day.

People still say they had the best day
when Nicky came out to play.

Sundays

Sundays are relaxing, like fishing in a
lake on a sunny summer day.

The comfort of the sun brings warmth to
the soul that is getting old.

Fish are lazy, but they are not crazy.

They are smart, but they are not too bright about art.

They are all taught to go to school, but in a
pool, and to leave their stools behind.

So if you are thinking of becoming a fish, they are better
thinkers in pools, but you won't be taught about art.

The Lady of the Night

The lady of the night that whispers sweet, soft sounds of
delight in my ear and I am out like a light.

As she watches me sleep, she can't believe the wonderful
sight, a man that cares with all his might.

He makes me mad; he makes me sad with
tears of joy and a heart of gold.

So I say, no more hanging on to fears of tears, and I will
listen to his sweet sounds that he whispers in my ear.

The times will tell when his whispers become a delight of
seeing things that appear out of sight.

Love, joy, and laughter are here to stay
to take over a broken heart.

Wonder of Life

When the wind blows, seeds of plants are planted in rows.

That miracles grow of wonder.

New seeds, smaller than a pinhead, grow high with slender sights, with beauty, and smells that are scenes swell.

We stand in awe and wonder: the beauty, grace, and peace.

A Child from a Mother

When we are young,

Mother teaches us to be kind and to share your dimes.

The times we spent sharing things with our mother, silly
jokes that come from older folks, from sharing our dreams
on what we want to be, leave a gleam on our face.

Mother's care is to see that she is always there.

Mother's troubles are always double, but this little
bubble was taught how to stay out of trouble.

Look, Mother, I am older and bolder; remember, Mother,
you taught me how to be kind, and I also share my dimes.

Thank you, Mother, for your time and being so kind.

August

August days are here for thirty-one days
to stay—hip-hip, hooray!

The sizzling sun makes travelling a lot of fun; some go
to Canada, some go to Cancun; the cheap travellers,
they just visit their neighbour's raccoon.

The sizzling heat is everywhere, even a few
surprises when you get there.

Your luggage gets lost and you turn into jaws.

You arrive at the Arctic, hoping to get out of the heat, but
instead, the Arctic is the hottest place to rest your head.

So you fly to Mexico just to find it is colder
there than the Arctic air.

Now your patience is getting thin, and so you tell your
brother Jim, who just got back from taking a cool swim.

You have one good day from the
two weeks that you were away.

Now, you are looking forward to coming
home and relaxing in your hometown.

The last night from your holiday, a tornado rips through
your town, and now it is nowhere to be found.

You cry with tears as big as crocodile tears; you are wet
from your nose to your toes, and then your wife says,

"Please don't scream, it is only a dream."

Birds of a Feather

As we sit and watch the birds of a feather,

We see big ones, little ones, colourful ones,

And ones that fly faster than an eagle in
Flight that is ready to take a bite.

They fly so fast and sometimes even crash.

They land with seattle grace just in the right place.

When the little birds swirl and twirl in flight,

They are faster than lightning without
the boom, just the zoom.

In your spare time, take a walk in the
park and watch the birds of a

Different feather control their flight,
and your fight with your troubles will

Slowly disappear into thin air.

A Child

A child born into the world of the unknown, a parent's
love for their child grows and protects all boundaries.

Lessons are learned, mistakes are made; love grows
like the branches, like a big old willow tree.

Protection from harm is an arm's length away as the
child grows, but the protection remains the same.

With the grace of God and the forgiving

For our mistakes, peace is seeded in the heart of a child
through the love that is received from the parents.

The love that spreads through one child is unknown
because love has no boundary.

The Arrow

The arrow is sharp and to my heart.

It goes through me and returns to you.

I feel less blue when I am with you.

Don't you feel that is true?

Your tender heart, caring love, and your
smiles make me tick for a long while.

In time, we will gaze at the stars; the space that
we will share will be bright as a shining light.

Roses

Roses are red, violets are blue,

I am so glad that I am with you.

Your laughter is sweet to hear, and
your smile can be seen from a mile.

May our hearts grow together to become one.

Let us stand together in this land with each other's hand.

When we take our vows, let us bow to each
other's love and fall into the well of love.

May

May is here: green, green grass is everywhere.

Flowers bloom with a big boom, different colours — red,
yellow, and blue—will put anybody in a better mood.

The different coloured flowers with sweet smells go
well with green, green grass that can be seen
from hillsides and valleys.

People's moods change from sad, mad, and into being glad.

The warmth of the sun puts people
in the mood for having fun.

May flowers from April showers will bring
you from being blue into a better mood.

June is here, and it is the time to
celebrate by singing a new tune.

Celebrations are everywhere: students are graduating,
and now their summer fun has just begun.

Hot, sizzling beaches put men at hand and ladies
tanning so gracefully, lying naked in the sand.

Parliaments is out, and they I want to shout because
they are singing a different tune in June.

July

Two weeks into summer, summer fun has just begun.

July is the time to get into nature, go for a run,
but don't get lazy and turn into a bum.

Cycle your way into town, there are always a few clowns
standing around; just smile and say good-bye, they
might ask for your money or your honey.

The summer is hot, so stay cool without acting like a fool;
go for a swim, but don't think you are going to get slim.

The nights are short, but the stars twinkle like lights that
is amazing; ponder your thoughts, but don't think a lot;
close your eyes and relax. Surrender your stress,
and your strain will be down the drain.

The hours will flow by, and before long, it will be dawn.

The new day will belong to you; plant a new seed from
your thoughts, make it grow, and watch it flow.

The month of July is your month to grow.

October

Fall season is in October, sun rays reflect colourful shades.

Treetops fill the sky with colours of red, orange, brown,
and green—makes a beautiful sight to be seen.

Fall breeze cools the warm late-summer air.

Quiet nights, too cold to sleep under the twinkling stars
that lie so far into the night skies from afar.

October is a time of different celebrations
—births, birthdays, and sometimes death.

There are wedding cakes and little ones playing patty-cake.

October is the time to shape our minds and body
for those cold days that are coming our way.

Thanksgiving Day

Thanksgiving Day is a time to give thanks; from past
reflections and the feast that we are about to have, good
memories from the feast will last longer than past defeats.

Laughter will linger like bees to honey;
love and forgiveness will spread.

In our hearts and mind, peace and forgiveness
stand tall like a mighty wall.

Those that forgive will have less pain to strain,
and their smile will fill the room like a giant balloon.

Thanksgiving Day comes once a year, but forgiving
people should come every day of the year.

To a Fine Lady

You are a lady of grace; your sweet smile, your laughter,
and your love is like a sweet white dove—soft to the touch.

When we spend time together, my heart beats
faster than the heartbeat of a running man.

Your style is cool, your hair is soft, your flair
overwhelms me with stares.

My heart throbs with happy beats;
I bow to my lady at her feet.

The tears of joy—love at last; may our love forever last.

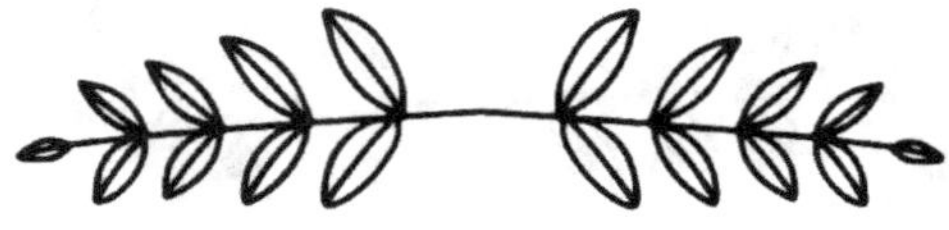

To My Dear Wife

I pray every day for our love to grow; our love is like a
little mustard seed, and it starts off slow but
will blossom in leaps and bounds.

We'll pray for better days when we don't see eye to eye
and later laugh on those good days.

We'll share our thoughts and plant a
few flowers in flowerpots.

We'll share our dreams in streams of thought,

We'll change each other's pot of gold,
for when we get old together, at least

We still have each other.

To My Sweet Daughter

To my sweet daughter,
who was born in time,
just in the nick of time.

Baby-blue eyes
and as beautiful as the twinkling
lights from the night sky.

As she got older, her bolder side grew too.

She was short in size, but her words
were quick as a whip.

Her love was soft like a morning white dove.

The times that we spent were special moments:
playing with her dolls and shopping at the malls.

She always got the latest doll, it was the best of them all.

To the Man I Love

To the man I love when he opens the door for me.

To the man I love when he gently kisses me.

To the man I love when he surprises me.

To the man I love that lifts me up with great pride.

To the man I love that puts joy in my soul.

To the man I love that will grow old with me.

I pray for his soul; when he is gone, his love will carry on.

A Man Called Winkles

There was a man called winkles; his hair was all crinkly.

He lived on the street with only a sheet.

His shoes were new; his eyes were blue,
and no one knew him.

His hands were wrinkly, and they smelled like pickles.

Before long he was singing a song that
everyone knew not to sing along; he would holler,

"Give me your dollar," and then he would be gone.

Some people said his name was Tom,
but in no time, people knew he would be gone.

He wanted to make money for his honey;
she knew that he wasn't a dear.

Before long he was gone with his
money, but not with his honey.

She was smart to go with

Art because she had a plan to get rid of her old man.

Tom knew how to screw people that he can, so I'll
keep the money, ditch the honey, and then he flew.

Not very long there was Tom singing his silly song,
but he changed his words and it went like this:
"My money is gone and so is my honey.

So I'll sing you a song so you can sing along with me.

Your money is evil, set it free, give it to me
—I'll set you free from your misery

Tom sings songs from day to day ,but
the pay goes straight to buying hay.

The Man with a Lost Shoe

Once upon a time, a man was invited to a wedding.

The timing was great because it was not too late to be wed.

The wedding was going to be small because of the hall.

The people were smart,they were sitting apart.

People were arriving from afar, but not by car.

Some took the bus, but not because of the guest.

The guest on the bus got a chill from being
thrilled because of the wedding.

The last of eight to be wed.

She was late in this world of eight; by now she is forty-two.

Now she is in the groove to move in style
for that long mile of marriage.

The man on the bus was thinking a lot, in a suit and shiny
shoes, to show what he can do for the move; to get in the
groove, he just loved his dancing shoes.

When he arrived, he was trying to get to his shoes, but one
slipped away and stayed on the bus for a longer ride.

So the one lonely shoe ended up on the bus to meet up with

Gus that only had one leg to stand on.

So when you have two shiny shoes, keep them apart
because someone with a big heart and
one leg will feel pretty smart.

Silence Sounds Of My Inner SOUL

I heard the sounds ringing aloud, then the feeling
of it lifted me up to a cloud.

Do Mighty sounds that rush through my soul tears of joy

Ringing like a fear to let go of those evil sounds.

I feel and hear those evil sounds dissipate like a
distance thunder.

The ringing of fear was ripping in the air , but then the
peaceful waves on the lake slowly ,slowly calmed my mind.

Peace has replace distress in my soul.

The sounds of waves of peace, is music to my ears,
comfort for my tears and washes all of my fears.

Now I stand in a flourished land , with tears of joy and love
at hand, being accepted through Gods grace,

I face no fear and silence rings with Angals sing .

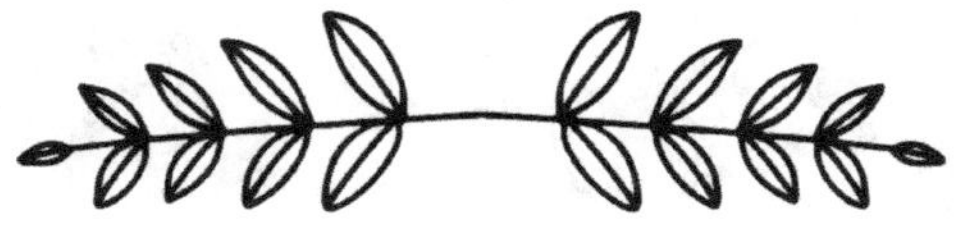

I stand in this land.

Then Angels take me by my the hand and walk me through
this promised land, where sounds of healing

Music fill the air and the contentment
that i felt was very rare.

Rare that it was because from conception, enters perception,
lies devil ways,but innocent ways, evil rings
in our minds and so does Gods whrisper ,
with truth, peace and loving kindness.

A brand new world you introduce me to, feel so inept.

As i reflect in the silence of my soul, of the journey
i have experienced, i now know that i am whole

www.ingramcontent.com/pod-product-compliance
Lightning Source LLC
Chambersburg PA
CBHW061346140726
47997CB00003B/1077